MW00957633

BLANK

Sketchbook

For Kids

Creative Learning Tools

Me in a wierd portrait!

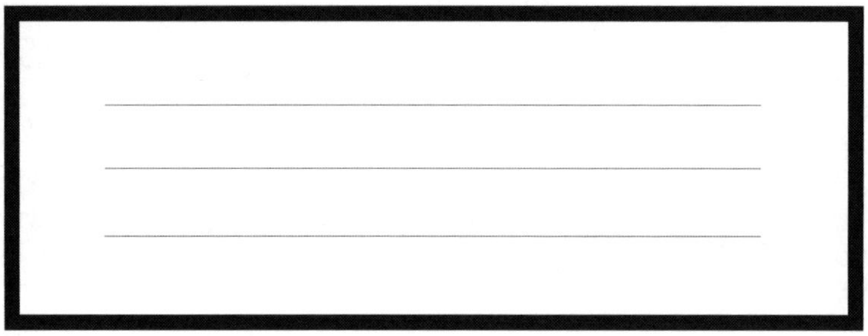

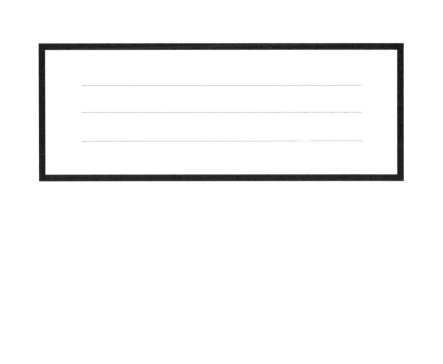

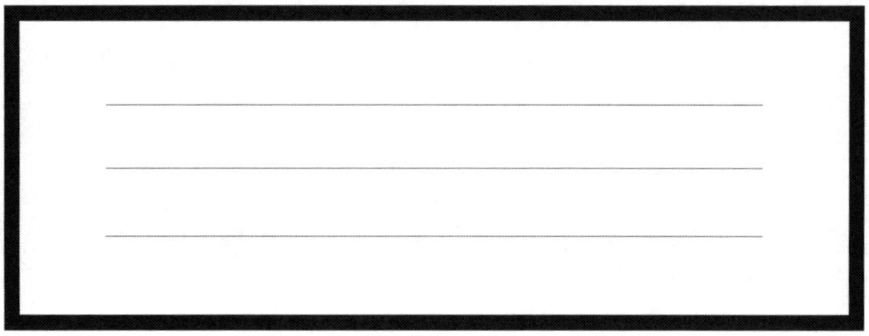

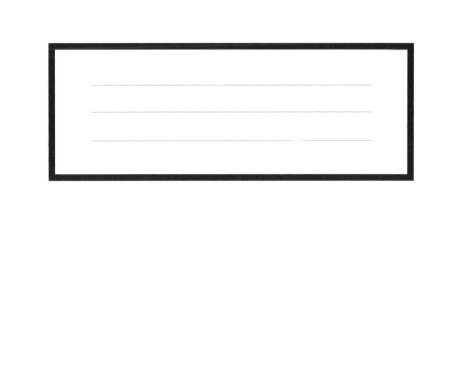

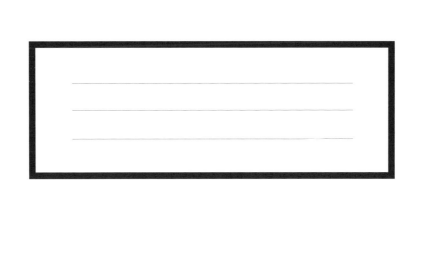

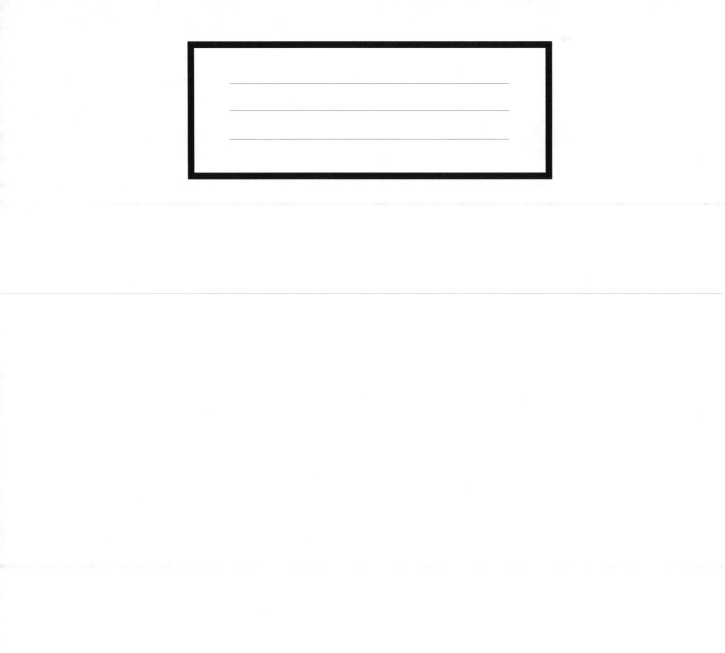

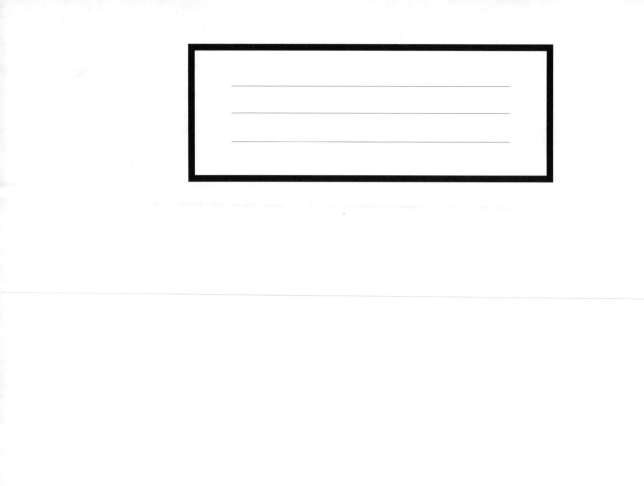

26550476R00057

Made in the USA
San Bernardino, CA
30 November 2015